Keesha's South African Adventure

by Cheril N. Clarke and Monica Bey-Clarke
Illustrated by Julia Selyutina

my family!
MyFamilyProducts.com

Copyright © 2016 by Cheril N. Clarke and Monica Bey-Clarke
Published by My Family! an imprint of Dodi Press

ALL RIGHTS RESERVED.

No part of this book may be reproduced in any form or by any electronic or mechanical means, including information storage and retrieval systems, without permission in writing from the publisher. The only exception is by a reviewer, who may quote short excerpts in a published review.

Published in the USA by My Family! an imprint of Dodi Press.
Printed in China.

www.MyFamilyProducts.com

ISBN: 978-0-9851067-5-1

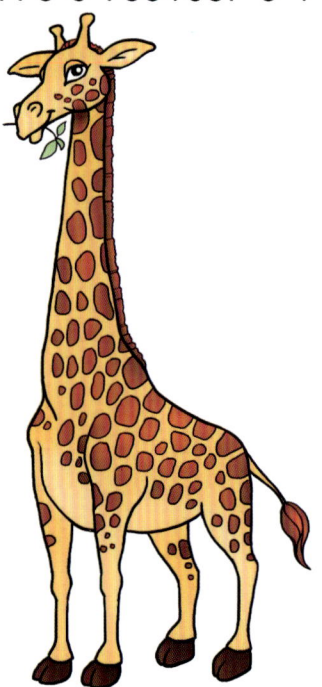

"Have fun at school, Keesha!" Momma and Mommy shouted from the bus stop.

"Bye!" Keesha waved before going to sit next to her best friend, Trevor.

"What do you think we're going to learn about today, Trevor?"

"I don't know, but I hope it's about dinosaurs or rocket ships!"

Keesha daydreamed about becoming an astronaut traveling to the moon in a shiny, red rocket ship.

When they got to school, Keesha and Trevor couldn't believe their eyes. Their teacher, Mrs. Apple, was dressed head to toe in safari gear!

"Good morning my fellow explorers," she announced. "Today, we're going to learn about another country. We're going to pretend we're on a safari in the beautiful country of South Africa."

Keesha couldn't contain her curiosity. "Where's that?" she blurted out.

Mrs. Apple spun a globe and pointed to the bottom of a big continent. "South Africa is a country on the continent of Africa. It touches the Atlantic Ocean on its west coast and the Indian Ocean on its east coast."

"Wow!" Trevor got excited.

"It's really hot there," Mrs. Apple continued, "kind of like having summer all year round. The best part is they have lots of animals we never get to see in the wild. They have lions, elephants, leopards, rhinoceroses…"

Keesha's imagination took off. Mrs. Apple kept talking, but all Keesha could think about was how much fun she would have if she visited South Africa instead of just pretending.

Mrs. Apple's cheerful voice interrupted Keesha's thoughts. "I'm going to choose my quietest listener to take home my friend Tau for the whole week," she said, holding up a stuffed toy lion.

Mrs. Apple chose Keesha!

When she got home from school, Keesha sat down to have a snack with Momma, Mommy, and Tau.

"What did you learn at school today?" Momma asked.

"We learned about South Africa! Mrs. Apple told us about all the animals that live there. I really want to see them! I was so good in school that I got to take home Tau for the whole week. We want to go on a safari together."

"Maybe one day, Keesha," Momma replied.

"Oh please, Mommy!" Keesha begged. "Maybe we can go for my birthday!"

As the weeks went by, Keesha couldn't stop thinking about South Africa.

On the morning of her birthday, Momma and Mommy came into her room with smiles on their faces and a big surprise for Keesha.

After they sang Happy Birthday, it was time for Keesha's gift. "Guess what, baby girl?" Momma said. "We're going to South Africa!"

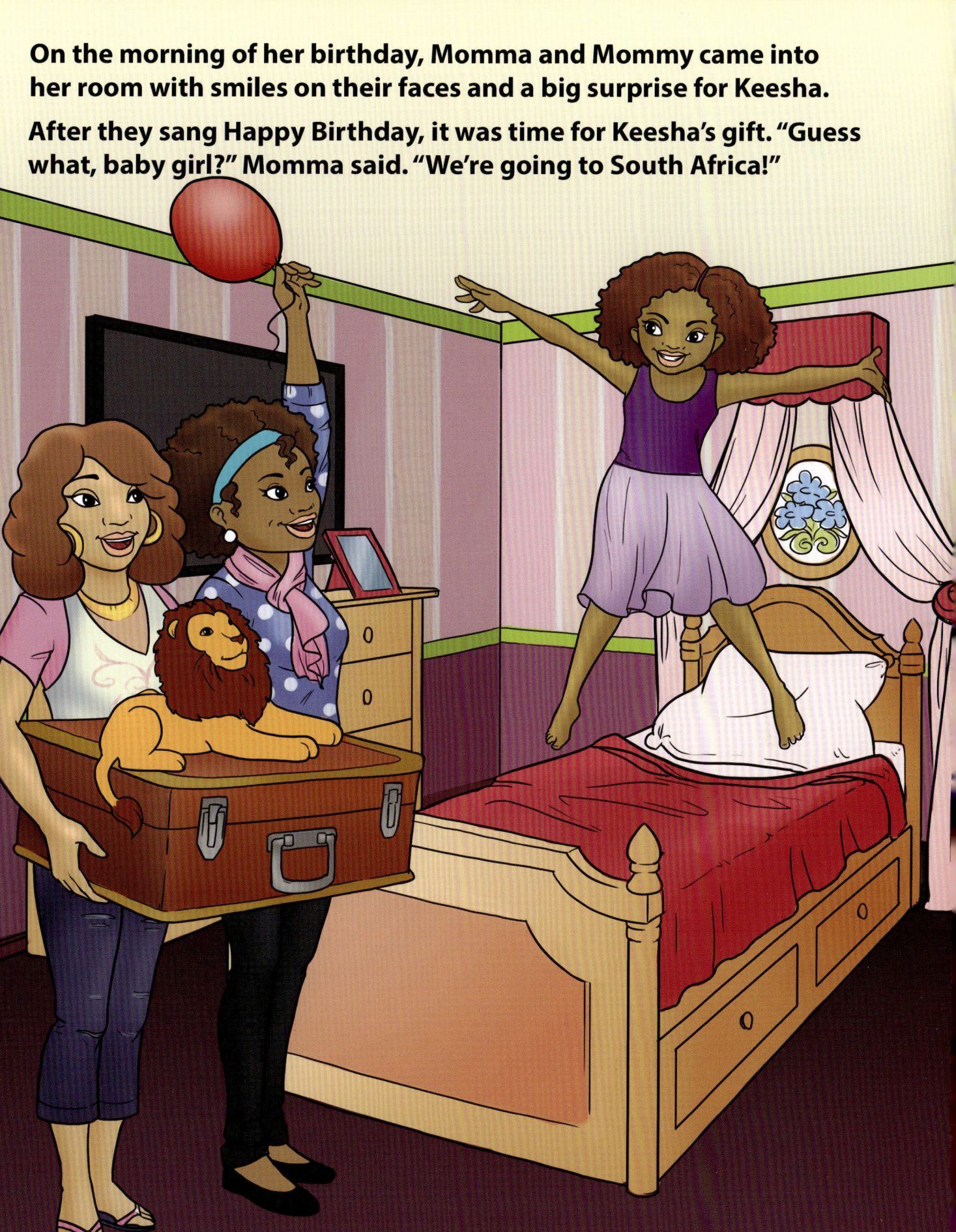

On the plane, Keesha wondered about the people she would meet. She wondered what types of food she would eat and thought about the animals she would see. She couldn't wait.

On their first night, Momma, Mommy, and Keesha attended their first braai, a South African barbeque. It seemed like a regular backyard barbeque, but it sure didn't taste like one! There weren't any hot dogs or hamburgers, and the South Africans used wood and charcoal to cook instead of gas. The meat was full of flavor.

A pontoon boat took them down a windy river on their second day. When Keesha saw hippopotamuses in the distance, she got scared because Mrs. Apple had told her class that hippos were one of the most dangerous animals in all of Africa. But the boat pilot kept them at a safe distance, and Keesha took some pictures that she looked forward to showing her friends at home.

On the third day, Momma, Mommy, and Keesha rode horses through an open plain filled with giraffes and wildebeests. The giraffes had big brown spots. Keesha loved the different patterns the spots made as they ran down the giraffes' long necks. The trail guide said that some of the giraffes were almost fourteen feet tall! Keesha and her moms got so close to one giraffe that they could almost pet it.

An adventure tour through Cango Caves was on their schedule for the fourth day. Keesha and her mommies crawled through tiny passages and over steep rocks to get through the ancient limestone caves. Keesha was so brave. The tour guide told them that the caves were discovered in 1780, more than 200 years earlier!

On the fifth day, Momma and Mommy wanted to shop at all the boutiques. Keesha thought she would be bored, but when she noticed a toymaker creating toy cars by hand, Keesha was fascinated. She stood and watched the woman for a while, impressed with the way the she could bend wires to make the different parts of the toy vehicle. *Trevor would really like one of these*, Keesha thought, so she asked her moms to buy one to give him as a gift

Keesha couldn't wait to swim at the beach on the sixth day. Standing at the shoreline, Keesha and her moms could even see whales swimming in the distance!

Keesha didn't think anything could top the activities of the previous six days, but on their last day in South Africa, Keesha and her mommies went on a safari! They saw so many different animals that Keesha's mouth hung open in awe during the entire adventure. They saw speedy cheetahs; huge, floppy-eared elephants; grazing buffalo; black and white striped zebras; and even few roaring lions!

On the plane ride home, Keesha couldn't control her enthusiasm... except when she was sleeping. She talked and slept, and talked and slept some more. It seemed to take forever to get home!

Before she went to bed, Keesha said, "Thank you so much, Momma and Mommy. You made my dreams come true! I can't wait to tell Trevor, Mrs. Apple, and all of my friends about this. They are never going to believe it!"

The next morning, Keesha woke up early to get dressed up just like a safari guide. When it was time for show-and-tell at school, she was the first one to raise her hand to participate. When Mrs. Apple called on Keesha, she ran to the front of the classroom and told her friends about her trip.

"Momma, Mommy, and I visited South Africa, and I saw so many wild animals! We traveled through dark and creepy caves, swam in pretty blue water, ate different foods like mealie bread and potato tarts, and met new people. I even brought back South African toys!"

"That's wonderful, Keesha!" Mrs. Apple said.

"Thank you for teaching us about South Africa, Mrs. Apple," Keesha responded. "Your lessons really made me want to go there. It was even more amazing than I thought it would be. I can't wait to find out what country you're going to teach us about next!"

Mrs. Apple was pleased. "You're welcome, Keesha. That's the great thing about learning; it makes you want to explore, try new activities, and meet new and exciting people."

"It sure does! I'm ready for my next adventure," Keesha squealed.

END!